C000051407

Publisher Details

This guide is published by Tax Insider Ltd, 3 Sanderson 3LN.

'101 Ways to Beat the Taxman' First published in July third edition May 2011, fourth edition April 2012.

Copyright

The right of Tax Insider Ltd and Sarah Bradford to be identified as the authors of this guide has been asserted in accordance with the Copyright, Designs and Patents Act 1988, England.

© 2010-2012 Tax Insider Ltd and Sarah Bradford

Trademarks

Tax Insider Ltd and other Tax Insider Ltd services/ products referenced in this guide are registered trademarks or trademarks of Tax Insider Ltd in the UK and/or other countries.

Disclaimer

1. This guide is produced for General guidance only, and professional advice should be sought before any decision is made. Individual circumstances can vary and therefore no responsibility can be accepted by Tax Insider, the co-author Sarah Bradford, or the publisher Tax Insider Ltd for any action taken or any decision made to refrain from action by any readers of this guide.

2. Tax rules and legislation are constantly changing and therefore the information printed in this guide is correct at the time of writing — March 2012

3. Neither the authors nor Tax Insider Ltd offer financial, legal or investment advice. If you require such advice then, we urge you to seek the opinion of an appropriate professional in the relevant field. We care about your success and therefore encourage you to take appropriate advice before you put any of your financial or other resources at risk. Don't forget, investment values can decrease as well as increase.

4. The content of this guide is for information only and professional advice should always be sought before undertaking any tax planning of any sort as individual circumstances vary and other considerations may have to be taken into account before acting.

5 To the fullest extent permitted by law Sarah Bradford and Tax Insider Ltd do not accept liability for any direct, indirect, special, consequential or other losses or damages of whatsoever kind arising from using this guide.

The guide itself is provided 'as is' without express or implied warranty.

Contents

Contents

Contents

Contents

1.   Individual Savings Accounts

Use your Individual Savings Account (ISA) allowance of each year.

For 2012/13 the limit is £11,280 (of which up to £5,640 can be invested in cash).

You can invest in cash, insurance, stocks and shares, etc. up to the limit each year and all proceeds are free from personal taxation. Investing at the start of each year maximises the tax-free return.

Using an ISA to invest £10,000 each year for ten years will provide a pot of £100,000 plus accumulated interest which is generating tax free returns.

Over a number of years this can be a viable alternative to a pension fund as proceeds can be taken at any time and there is no requirement to wait for retirement age or to take an annuity.

These ISAs are also useful for the retention of income within the fund as this is received effectively tax free.

This means that the fund can grow at a faster rate than if the funds were held outside of an ISA where potentially 40% or 50% of the investment return would be taxed.

Individual Savings Account

John invests £7,000 into shares using his ISA.

After three years, this has grown to £14,000, and he decides to cash it in.

He has used his annual capital gains tax allowance elsewhere.

The amount of tax he pays on the gain is NIL.

However, if he had made the investment outside an ISA, purchasing shares in his own name, he would pay capital gains tax on the gain of £7,000.

If he is a higher rate taxpayer, he would face a capital gains tax bill of £1,960 (£7,000 @ 28%).

2. Junior ISAs

Use your children's Junior ISA limit.

Junior ISAs were launched on 1 November 2011. Junior ISAs are long-term savings accounts for children. A child can have a junior ISA if he or she is under 18, lives in the UK or does not have a child trust fund account.

The money belongs to the child, although anyone can put money in. There are two types of junior ISA – cash Junior ISA and a stocks and shares Junior ISA. A child can have one or both.

The maximum amount that can be paid into a Junior ISA is £3,600 a year. Income and gains are tax-free. Except in very limited circumstances the money cannot be withdrawn until the child is 18. An ISA can be used to build up a nice savings pot for the child or maybe to fund university or college.

Once a child reaches 16, they can open an adult cash ISA and take advantage of the investment limits.

Junior ISAs

David invests £3,000 a year for the next 18 years into a Junior ISA for his baby daughter Lucy. When Lucy reaches 18, she will have a fund of £54,000 plus accumulated interest.

The interest is tax-free and is not taxed as David's income.

---

3. Bank And Building Society Interest

If you are a non-taxpayer, make sure you claim back any tax paid on interest earned on bank and building society deposits.

To receive interest gross in future you should complete the Inland Revenue form R40.

You can download the form via the following link:

http://www.hmrc.gov.uk/forms/r40.pdf

Bank and Building Society Interest

John holds £50,000 on deposit and receives interest of £2,000 net of 20% tax.

He has no other income for the year.

He is therefore entitled to reclaim the £500 tax deducted from his interest by utilising his personal allowance against this income.

Also in future years he should file form R40 to receive the interest gross.

---

4. Use Non-Taxpayers' Personal Allowances

If one spouse or civil partner is working and the other has no taxable income, it is worthwhile considering transferring income-producing investments to the non-working spouse/civil partner in order to utilise their personal allowance.

This will save tax on the income and will increase the overall return from these investments.

This can be particularly useful with even the smallest amounts of savings.

Use Non-Taxpayers Allowances

Mr & Mrs Smith have £10,000 in savings. The entire amount is held in Mr Smith's sole name.

Mr Smith is a higher rate taxpayer and pays tax at 40%, and Mrs Smith does not work and has no taxable income.

At present, the interest received of £500 suffers tax at 40%, leaving a net amount received of £300.

By transferring this money into an account in Mrs Smith's name and utilising her personal allowance, the interest can be received free of tax.

This means that an instant tax saving of £200 can be made.

5.   Dividends And Non-Taxpayers

Dividends are received with a non-refundable 10% tax credit.

Because this cannot be reclaimed by non-taxpayers, it is worthwhile considering changing investments so as to receive savings income, such as bank or building society interest, rather than dividends.

This is because bank and building society interest suffers a 20% tax deduction, which can be claimed back by a non-taxpayer.

Non-taxpayers can also register to receive bank and building society interest gross (see Tip 3).

The ability to receive the full amount of savings income can be very important for pensioners on low incomes relying on their investments to generate income in retirement.

Dividends and Non-Taxpayers

Mr & Mrs Smith have built up a portfolio of investments, which currently yield £9,900 (gross) per annum in dividends.

They are all received with a 10% tax credit, which leaves a net income of £8,910.

By switching their investment strategy, (say by investing in Government Stock), they now receive gross income of £9,900 with a 20% tax deduction. This leaves them with a net income of £7,920.

By filing tax repayment claims and utilising their personal allowances, they receive back the £1,980 tax deducted and are left with a net income of £9,900.

This means that they are better off by £990 (or 10%).

This can be a very significant amount of money, especially for those on low incomes.

6.   Utilising Your Annual CGT Exemption

If you have significant capital gains within your portfolio then it is important to utilise the annual capital gains tax allowance.

For the 2012/13 tax year this is worth £10,600 per person, and is one of the most generous annual allowances in the world.

Any disposals within this figure are exempt from capital gains tax.

This means that you can use your tax-free allowance each year by selling off just enough shares (or other qualifying assets) to realise a gain equivalent to the annual exemption.

Utilising this exemption could also significantly boost your overall return over a number of years.

Please note that this allowance does not carry forward. So this means that if it is not used in the tax year then it is lost!

To view the allowances for previous years please use this link: http://www.hmrc.gov.uk/rates/cgt.htm

Using your Annual CGT Allowance

Smart John

John has a significant share portfolio and is a higher rate taxpayer.

For 2012/13 he will be liable to capital gains tax at 28% on any gains in excess of his personal allowance.

He has held these shares for a number of years, and has always made use of his annual exemption for capital gains tax purposes, selling sufficient shares to realise a gain approximately equal to the capital gains tax exempt amount (£10,600 for 2012/13).

By utilising his annual exemption for 2012/13 he is saving £10,600 @ 28% = £2,968 in tax.

This means that as a result of using his annual exemption each year and only making disposals within the annual exemption rather than disposing of his shares all in one go, he is much better off as any gains on the shares are realised tax-free.

Not so Smart Jack

Jack doesn't use his annual exemption and sells off shares and realises gains of £25,000 in2012/13.

He has other income of £50,000.

As he is a higher rate taxpayer, he pays capital gains tax at 28%.

The annual exemption of £10,600 is set against the gain of £25,000, leaving net chargeable gains of £14,400. He pays tax on these gains of £4,032 (£14,400 @ 20%), leaving him with £20,968 after tax to reinvest.

Compare this with John, who realised his gains completely tax free by selling his shares over a number of years and making best use of the annual allowance. As a result, John is 16% better off than Jack.

7. Utilising Your Spouse's Or Civil Partner's Annual CGT Exemption

By transferring assets into joint names prior to sale, you can utilise your spouse's or civil partner's annual exemption as well as your own if he or she has not used it. For 2012/13 the annual exemption is £10,600 which means that a couple can make gains of up to £21,200 before paying any capital gains tax.

Transfers between spouses and civil partners are treated as a no gain/no loss transaction and hence the spouse/civil partner steps into the shoes of the other holder, taking over their base cost and length of ownership.

This can be especially useful when selling investment properties, although stamp duty land tax considerations need to be taken into account.

Utilising Spouse's/Civil Partner's CGT Allowance

Mr Smith (a higher rate taxpayer) sells shares in 2012/13 and realises a taxable gain of £20,200.

He utilises his annual exemption and pays tax on £9,600@ 28% = £2,688.

If Mr Smith had transferred the ownership into joint names prior to the sale then Mr & Mrs Smith would each have a taxable gain of £10,100, which would be covered by the annual exemption of £10,600.

By using their annual exemptions (£10,600 each) they would incur no tax on this gain, thus leaving them £2,688 better off.

---

8.   Pension Funding

Payments into an approved pension scheme attract tax relief at your highest rate of tax and are deemed to be paid net of basic rate tax.

From 2011/12 the annual limit on tax relieved pension savings has been reduced from £255,000 to £50,000. However, relief is still given at the taxpayer's marginal rate of tax, meaning that pension contributions still remain tax-effective for higher and additional rate tax payers.

The ability to utilise unused allowances from the previous three tax years (subject to a cap of £50,000 on tax relieved pension savings where allowances are brought forward for years from before 2011/12) means that it is still possible to make significant tax-relieved contributions to a registered pension scheme (£200,000 over a four-year period).

A basic rate taxpayer will effectively pay £80 for a £100 contribution into a registered pension scheme. For higher rate taxpayers, a £100 pension contribution costs £60 and for additional rate taxpayers, the cost is just £50. This makes pension savings particularly tax-efficient.

Pension Funding

John invests £2,000 into his pension scheme, which costs him £1,600 as this is paid net of basic rate tax, which the pension fund recovers bringing the pension contribution to £2,000.

As a higher rate taxpayer paying tax at 40% he claims higher rate tax relief on this and receives a tax rebate of £400 from HMRC.

The £400 arises as a result of reclaiming the difference between the basic (20%) and higher rates of tax (40%), i.e. 20% of £2,000, or £400.

Jack is an additional rate taxpayer paying tax at 50%. He too invests £2,000 into his pension scheme, which cost his £1,600 as this is paid net of basic rate tax.

As an additional rate taxpayer he can claim tax relief of £600 from HMRC, which he receives as a tax rebate.

This is 30% of £2,000, being the difference between the basic rate (20%) and the additional rate of 50%.

9. Making The Most Of Pension Tax Relief at 50%

In his March 2012 Budget the Chancellor announced that the additional rate of tax is to be reduced to 45% from 6 April 2013.

Additional rate taxpayers should make the most of the opportunity to receive pension tax relief at 50%. Tax relief is available on contributions up to the annual allowance. To the extent it is unused the annual allowance can be carried forward for up to three years.

This means that where no contributions have been made in the previous three years it is possible to make tax relieved contributions of up to £200,000 (earnings permitting) in 2012/13.

A £50,000 contribution to a registered pension scheme will cost an additional rate tax £25,000 in 2013/14. However, with the reduction in the additional rate to 45% from 2013/14, a £50,000 contribution will cost an additional rate taxpayer £27,500 in 2013/14.

Making the most of pension tax relief at 50%

Paul is an additional rate taxpayer. In 2012/13 he has earnings of £800,000. He has not made a contribution to a registered pension scheme for five years. He has annual allowances of £50,000 carried forward from 2011/12, 2010/11 and 2009/10 available to him, as well as his annual allowance of £50,000 for 2012/13 – a total of £200,000.

He makes a contribution to a registered pension scheme of £200,000 in 2012/13. The contribution is paid net of basic rate tax, so Paul pays £160,000 into the pension scheme.

He claim a further £60,000 tax relief via his self-assessment return, being the difference between the basic rate and the additional rate (30% of £200,000 = £60,000).

The £200,000 contribution costs him £100,000.

If he waits until 2013/14 to make the contribution, it will cost him £110,000, as he will receive tax relief at 40% rather than at 50%. Taking advantage of the opportunity to receive pension tax relief at 50% has saved him £10,000.

10. Making Pension Contributions On Behalf Of Non-Working Partners And Children

Most people are unaware that the Government allows contributions of up to £3,600 gross (£2,880 net of basic rate tax) into a pension scheme regardless of your level of income or age.

So if you want you can contribute into a pension scheme for your non-working spouse, children, etc., and they are deemed to have made the contribution net of basic rate tax even if they are non-taxpayers.

Advanced Pension Funding

John wishes to increase his family's pension fund at retirement and makes a contribution of £2,880 into his non-working wife's pension fund.

This is worth £3,600 in the scheme and is able to obtain a tax saving of £720 by doing so.

He also contributes £2,880 into each of his three children's pension schemes which again is worth £3,600 in each of their schemes, receiving a further £720 tax advantage in each scheme (£2,160 in total).

As the children will have their pension scheme running for much longer than someone who does not start a pension until they start work, they will have a considerably bigger pension fund at retirement than, say, someone starting their pension funding at the typical age of 30.

11.   Invest In A Venture Capital Trust

If your attitude to investment risk is at the higher end of the scale then you could invest in a venture capital trust (VCT). These are designed to encourage investment into smaller higher-risk trading companies.

These have significant tax benefits as they allow you to defer capital gains tax liabilities and attract income tax relief at 30% on your investment.

Three significant benefits of investing money into a VCT are:

- No Capital Gains Tax is paid until the shares are sold,
- Dividends are received tax free and
- No CGT is payable within the trust.

Invest in A Venture Capital Trust

John invests £10,000 into a VCT.

He receives a £3,000 tax rebate after submitting his Tax Return, which is the equivalent of 30% of his investment.

12. Invest In An Enterprise Investment Scheme (EIS)

EIS schemes offer tax relief on contributions at 30% and a tax deferral on gains. EIS investments are generally high risk and invest in a single company.

If the investment is into your own company, only CGT deferral relief is available.

Investing in an EIS

John and EIS

John decides to set up a new trading business and subscribes for £50,000 of shares at par, and has gains realised elsewhere of £50,000 which he invests in the shares.

The company qualifies for EIS treatment and he applies for an EIS scheme number. He elects to defer the gains into the new shares, and saves having to pay capital gains tax on his gains.

This gives him a tax deferral of £14,000 (28% of £50,000)!

Alisha and EIS

Alisha invests £50,000 into a qualifying EIS company in 2012/13 with which she has no connection.

She has gains of £50,000 for the year which she invests in the EIS. She defers the tax payable on her gains of £14,000 and also receives a tax rebate of 30% of her contribution, i.e. £15,000.

This makes a total effective rate of relief on her investment a massive 48%.

---

13.   Age-Related Tax Allowances

In his 2012 Budget, in a measure dubbed `the granny tax' the Chancellor revealed plans to phase-out the age-related element of the personal allowance by freezing the age-related allowances from April 2013 until the basic personal allowance catches up. However, age-related allowances remain available for the time being.

For 2012/13 and earlier years, higher personal allowances are available to persons aged over 65 (with a higher allowance still applying to those aged over 75).The age-related personal allowance for 2013/14 for persons aged 65 to 74 is £10,500 and that for persons aged 75 and over is £10,660.

However anyone over the age of 65 needs to be aware that the age-related enhancement is gradually reduced where income exceeds the income limit for the tax year in question. For 2012/13 the age-related income is restricted once income exceeds £25,400.The restriction is an abatement of the relief of £1 for every £2 of income above this limit until the allowance is reduced to the level of the standard personal allowance (£8,105 for 2012/13). The abatement rules mean that you lose £1 of the allowance for every additional £2 of income, resulting in a very high effective tax rate on income just above the limit.

The age-related element of the allowance is fully abated for taxpayers aged 65 to 74 who have income for 2012/13 of £30,190 and above and for taxpayers aged 75 and above who have income of £30,510 and above.

Care should be taken to ensure income producing assets are held in the most tax efficient manner to preserve entitlement to the higher age-related allowances where possible. This may mean transferring assets between spouses/civil partners to keep income of one partner below the abatement limit. Where only one partner is entitled to the age-related allowance, the aim is to keep that partner's income below the abatement limit and where both partners have age-related allowances, if one is entitled to the higher allowance (aged 75 plus), his or her income should if possible be kept below the abatement limit.

For 2013/14, the age-related allowance for people age 65 to 74 will be restricted to people born after 5 April 1938 but before 6 April 1948 and the age-related allowance for those aged 75 over will be restricted to those born before 6 April 1938. The allowances will remain at their 2012/13 levels.

Age-related Tax Allowances

Mr & Mrs Smith are 70 years old.

Mr Smith has income of £40,000, and Mrs Smith has no income whatsoever.

Mr Smith would be entitled to the age-related allowance for 2012/13 for persons aged 65 to 74 of £10,500. However, as Mrs Smith has no income the allowance would be wasted.

As Mr Smith has income in excess of £30,190, the age-related portion of his allowance would be fully abated such that he receives the standard personal allowance for 2012/13 of £8,105.

By redistributing the income producing assets so that for 2012/13 they both had income of at least £10,500 but below £25,499 Mr & Mrs Smith could gain full use of their age related allowance.

By doing this they will benefit from combined personal allowances of £21,000 as compared to £8,105 prior to the income redistribution. This will save tax for 2012/13 of £2,579 ((£21,000 - £8,105) x 20%).

14. Keeping The Full Personal Allowance

The basic personal allowance is reduced where a person has 'net adjusted income' in excess of £100,000. The personal allowance (£8,105 for 2012/13) is reduced by £1 for every £2 by which this limit is exceeded until the allowance is fully abated.

This means that anyone with income of more than £116,210 loses all their personal allowance.

By redistributing income to a lower income spouse or civil partner, for example by putting investments in the spouse's or civil partner's name only, so as to reduce income below £100,000 the allowance can be preserved.

Likewise, adjusted net income can be reduced by making pension contributions, which is in itself beneficial due to the higher rate relief that they receive. Charitable donations would also work (although the donator would lose the benefit of the donation).

Keeping the Full Personal Allowance

John has adjusted net income of £120,000 for 2012/13, of which £30,000 is in the form of interest from investments. His wife has income of £10,000 for the year.

As John has income in excess of £116,210, he will lose the personal allowance for 2012/13. By transferring the investments to his wife, his income is reduced to £90,000 and he retains the personal allowance.

For a higher rate taxpayer paying tax at 40% the personal allowance is worth £3,242 for 2012/13 (8,105 @ £40%). By transferring income to his wife John retains the personal allowance, saving £3,242. As the income transferred to his wife is taxed at 20% rather than at 40%, the couple save a further £6,000 in tax (see the next Tip).

15. Equalising Marginal Rates Of Tax

For 2012/13 there are three rates of income tax – the basic rate of 20%, the higher rate of 40% and the additional rate of 50%.

By transferring income to a lower earning spouse or civil partner it is possible to save tax at the higher rates, thereby reducing the combined tax bill.

Equalising Marginal Rates of Tax

John is an additional rate taxpayer with income (after deducting the personal allowance) of £170,000.

His wife has income (after deducting personal allowances) of £50,000.

By transferring income of £20,000 to his wife, the marginal rate of tax is reduced from 50% to 40%, saving tax of £2,000 (10% of £20,000).

A word of caution, where it is not possible to reduce income below £100,000 for both partners to preserve personal allowances, care should be taken to avoid the high marginal rates.

If John's wife had been a basic rate taxpayer, the saving would have been £6,000 (30% of £20,000). It would have then been advisable to transfer sufficient income to fully utilise her basic rate band. For example, if she had income of £10,000 for 2012/13, to fully utilise her basic rate band, John should transfer income of £32,997 to his wife, which will bring her income up to the higher rate limit of £42,475 for 2012/13.

Equalising income where possible will ensure that personal allowances and lower tax bands are not wasted.

---

16. Bonus/Dividend Timing

Simply by timing the payment of dividends and bonuses from your own company you can save a considerable amount of tax or delay tax payments by up to a year. With the reduction in the additional rate of tax from 50% to 45% from 6 April 2013, this can potentially save tax as well as delaying the payment date. The dividend additional rate is 42.5% for 2012/13, but falls to 37.5% for 2013/14.

Bonus/Dividend Timing

Lisa runs her own company, Lisa Ltd.

By paying a dividend on 6 April 2013 instead of 5 April 2013 she delays the payment of higher rate tax on this dividend by twelve months.

If she is an additional rate taxpayer, delaying the payment by one day will also save tax. If paid on 5 April 2013, the dividend will attract tax at the dividend additional rate of 42.5%. If payment is delayed until 6 April, the dividend is taxed at the dividend additional rate for 2013/14 of 37.5%.

17. Dividends - Below The Higher Rate Threshold

If you do not need the income or wish to build up funds within the company, restricting dividends paid to just below the higher rate threshold can save considerable amounts of tax.

Dividends Below the Higher Rate Threshold

John does not need more than £30,000 per annum to live on so pays dividends just below the higher rate threshold (£42, 475 for 2012/13)).

By doing this, John does not need to pay any tax on the dividends as the liability at the dividend ordinary rate of 10% is matched by the associated tax credit.

The tax cost is the corporation tax paid on the funds at a rate of 20% (assuming John's company pays corporation tax at the small profits rate (20% for the financial year 2012).

18.   Fluctuating Dividends

By fluctuating the payment of dividends so as to pay a large dividend one year and a small dividend the following year, it is possible to avoid having to make payments on account, which achieves a cashflow advantage by delaying the date on which tax is due.

Fluctuating dividends

John is a higher rate taxpayer, and aims to draw out £50,000 per annum on average in dividends from his company.

By fluctuating the amount of dividends and only drawing out sufficient dividends to take advantage of the basic rate tax band in alternate years, he can avoid paying payments on account and hence achieve a cash flow advantage.

Assume he withdrew £30,000 in dividends in 2011/12 and this was his only income.

As there is no tax to pay, for 2011/12 payments on account are not due for2012/13.

If he pays dividends of £80,000 in 2012/13, the higher rate liability will not be due until 31 January 2014 (rather than in equal instalments on 31 January 2013 and 31 July 2013 had he paid dividends of £50,000 in each tax year).

---

19.   Company Cars – The CO_2 Rating

Because the car benefit charge and fuel scale charge are linked to the carbon dioxide emissions from the car, consider changing to a lower emission car and you can save considerable amounts in tax.

For more detailed information and the tax rates please click on the following link www.hmrc.gov.uk/cars/index.htm to open the guidance on the HMRC website.

Company Cars – the CO_2 Rating

Bill is a higher rate tax payer and pays tax at 40%. He works for ABC Ltd. He has a company car, which is available for private use.

By switching from a car with an emission rating of 210 g/km to one with a rating of 135 g/km, the tax charge on a £20,000 list price car changes from £6,600 (33% of £20,000) to £3,600 (18% of £20,000) (2012/13 figures).

The reduction in the benefit reduces the tax payable from £2,640 (£6,600 @ 40%) to £1,440 (£3,600 @ 40%) and saves tax of £1,200.

If fuel is also provided, the fuel benefit would be reduced from £6,666 (33% of £20,200) to £3,636, reducing the tax payable on the car fuel from £2,666.40 (£6,666 @ 40%) to £1,454,40 (£3,636 @ 40%), saving further tax of £1,212 .The employer would also save Class 1A National Insurance contributions of £418.14.

By choosing a car with actual CO_2 emissions of less than 75 g/km, the percentage of the list price taxed falls to 5%.

---

20.   Company Cars – Tax-Free Electric Cars

By choosing an electric car it is possible to have a company car tax-free as zero-emission cars have a zero charge for five years from 2010/11. However, the charge on zero-emissions cars is due to increase to 13% from 2015/16 and to 15% from 2016/17, so the opportunity for a tax-free electric company is for a limited period only.

> **Company Cars – Tax-Free Electric Cars**
>
> Mark is a higher rate taxpayer.
>
> By choosing an electric car which has zero emissions he is able to enjoy the benefit of a company car tax free up to an including 2014/15. This can generate considerable savings. For example, if instead he chose a car costing £30,000 with CO_2 emissions of 195g/km, for 2012/13 he would be taxed on 30% of the list price, i.e. £9,000. At 40%, the tax payable would be £3,600.

21. Company Car Or Car Allowance?

Company cars are highly taxed and the tax burden is due to increase in future years as emissions criteria are made stricter, raising the appropriate percentage. Therefore, you should consider whether it would be more appropriate to use your own vehicle for company business.

If you decide to do this then you can claim a car allowance and mileage rate for business miles.

Depending on miles covered and the type of car, this can save a considerable amount of tax.

It also has the advantage that if you move jobs you don't have to hand the car back.

Company Car or Car Allowance?

Bill has a company car and pays tax on a total of £9,500 in benefit charges. He pays tax at 40%. The tax cost of having a company car is £3,800.

He travels 10,000 miles per annum on business, and the company offers him a car allowance of £6,000 per annum instead of his company car.

By taking the allowance and providing his own car, he immediately saves £3,800 in tax on the benefit charge and gains another £3,480 from the car allowance (£6,000 less tax of £2,400 and National Insurance contributions of £120).

He is also able to claim £4,500 per annum tax free mileage allowance at 45p per mile, leaving him potentially much better off (although this will depend on the type of vehicle and method of purchase).

22.   Employ Your Family

If a member of your family has no income, you could employ them in your business or take them into partnership, and save a significant amount of tax for the family as a whole.

Care must be taken to ensure that the arrangement is commercial and the level of pay is commensurate with the duties performed to avoid an attack from HMRC.

The National Minimum Wage rules also need to be considered, although the National Minimum Wage does not apply to directors.

Employing Your Family

John's wife Kelly has no income, but spends a considerable amount of time answering the telephone in John's home office and dealing with correspondence.

She also has the task of keeping track of the accounts, for which she is not paid.

By bringing her into a partnership or paying her a salary he can reduce his own exposure to higher rate tax and reward her for the efforts she puts in on behalf of the business.

This simple strategy can save several thousand pounds in tax along the way.

23. Income From A Family Trust

If you have a family trust with discretionary powers, consider making payments to your children.

Trusts are a complex area and advice should always be sought but it is possible to utilise the children's tax free personal allowance in this way.

In fact, these payments can be combined with the pension payments point discussed previously to make a double saving.

Income from a Family Trust

John's family have a family trust, and it makes payments net of the trust rate of tax (50%) equivalent to the annual personal allowance of £8,105 gross per annum (2012/13 figures).

The tax paid by the trust of £4,052 is recovered by the children by making a repayment claim. £2,880 net (£3,600 gross) is paid into a pension scheme on their behalf, resulting in a further tax advantage of £720 per child.

24. Children's Income

Income earned from gifts from parents is exempt if less than £100 per annum. Otherwise the income is taxable as that of the parents.

Consider gifting sufficient capital to generate this amount in income or utilise tax exempt savings products to build up savings for the children.

This limit can be overcome by putting money into a Junior ISA (see Tip 2) or by investing in Children's Bonds, which generate a tax-free return.

Gifts can be made by grandparents to grandchildren without restriction.

Children's Income
John is a higher rate taxpayer (paying tax at 40%) and gifts each of his children £2,000, which is placed in a children's account for them and earns £80 interest per annum. As this is less than £100 it is not taxed as John's income. John therefore saves £32 per annum in tax which he would have otherwise paid on the interest income had the money been placed in an account in his own name.

25.   Claim Your Tax Credits

A large number of people are entitled to either one or both of the child tax credit and the working families' tax credit.

Eligibility can easily be checked by going to the HMRC website (www.hmrc.gov.uk/taxcredits/index.htm). This can be worth several thousand pounds per annum for low income families.

Tax Credits

John and Kelly live together and have a combined income of £12,000 with two children under 16 years old.

By claiming children's tax credit and working families tax credits they will receive a considerable sum of money, which will be of enormous benefit to them, all for the time taken to complete the claim form.

26.   Take Your Tax – Free Lump Sum

By taking the lump sum option offered on most personal pension schemes you receive a tax-free lump sum and purchase an annuity with the balance.

Because the annuity is taxable whereas the lump sum is not (as long as it does not exceed 25% of the pension fund), you can be considerably better off from a tax viewpoint by taking the lump sum.

Take Your Tax – Free Lump Sum

Upon retirement Alex is offered the choice of:

- a straightforward annuity for his pension fund of £100,000 of £6,000 per year, or

- a lump sum of £25,000 and an annuity of £5,000 per year.

By taking the latter lump sum option he saves tax yearly on the amount of the annuity forgone.

He also has the opportunity to invest the lump sum to generate additional income (although any income earned may be taxable in its own right depending on the nature of the investment).

---

27. State Pension Entitlement

To maximise your state pension, ensure that the National Insurance record is up to date.

About four months before you reach state retirement age you will receive a form from the Government showing you what you are entitled to.

When you receive this it will also be possible to purchase additional years if the last few years of your working life have not made sufficient contributions to entitle you to the full pension.

This can be very worthwhile with a typical payback time of around five years.

However, it should be noted that the number of years' contributions needed to qualify for a full state is now 30.

Therefore you should check carefully that any additional contributions are worthwhile, as for many their contribution record will be sufficient.

State Pension Entitlement

John is 64 years old and is about to take his state pension in the following year.

He enquires as to the state of his contribution record and discovers that by paying £400 for each of the last five years (as his earnings have been very low) he can increase his state pension entitlement by £80 per annum of each year.

Therefore with a net cost investment of £2,000 he will receive an additional £400 per annum for the rest of his life.

This means that, he will be in profit if he survives for more than five years, and this will be index linked income as well.

28. Stop Paying National Insurance

Once you have reached retirement age, you are no longer liable to pay employee's National Insurance Contributions (NIC) (although liability to employer's contributions continues).

For the self-employed, you do not pay NIC after the 5th April following your attainment of the state retirement age.

> **Stop Paying National Insurance**
>
> John has been paying himself a salary of £30,000 per annum from his company, and continues to work beyond state retirement age.
>
> He is no longer liable to employee's NIC and hence is some £2,687.40a year better off (2012/13figures).

29. Quarterly PAYE Payments

For employers, an important cash flow advantage can be obtained by making PAYE payments quarterly rather than monthly.

This is a choice employers have, provided their payments do not exceed £1,500 per month.

Quarterly PAYE Payments

John has one full time employee, and his total PAYE deductions per month average less than £1,500.

He chooses to pay by quarterly instalments and hence has the use of up to £4,500 for a couple of months.

This can be a very useful payment strategy when money may be tight.

30. Pay PAYE On Time To Avoid Penalties

Penalties are charged if PAYE is paid late on more than one occasion in the tax year.

The penalty charged for late payment is a percentage of the PAYE paid late.

The penalty rate is linked to the number of occasions on which payment was made late in the tax year, ranging from 1% if payment is made late on two, three or four occasion in the year to 4% if payment is made late on 11 or 12 occasions.

A further penalty of 5% is charged if payment is outstanding after six months. If payment remains due after 12 months, a subsequent 5% penalty is levied.

A PAYE month runs to the 5th of each month. Payments of PAYE and NIC must reach HMRC by 19th month if paid by cheque.

Where payment is made electronically, cleared funds must reach HMRC's bank account by 22nd month.

But see Tip 31 below where the normal payment date falls on a weekend or bank holiday.

31.   Allow For Bank Holidays And Weekends When Making Payments Of PAYE

As highlighted in tip 30, PAYE should be paid on time each month to avoid late payment penalties.

However, to avoid getting caught out by bank holidays and weekends, ensure that payment is made early when the normal payments day falls on a bank holiday or a weekend, When this happens, the payment (or in the case of electronic payments, cleared funds) must reach HMRC by the last working day before the bank holiday or weekend on which the normal payment day falls.

In2012/13, where payment is not made electronically (so must reach HMRC by 19th month), payment should be made early in May 2012, August 2012 and January 2013 to allow for the fact that the 19th falls on a weekend.

Where payment is made electronically, payment should be sent early in July 2012, September 2012 and December 2012 to allow for the fact that the 22nd falls on a weekend.

Allow for bank holidays and weekends when making payments of PAYE

John pays his PAYE by cheque each month, posting the cheque on the 16th month to allow sufficient time for posting. His payment for PAYE month 1 (month to 5 May2012) must reach HMRC by 19 May 2012 .

However, as this falls on his Saturday, in reality it must reach HMRC the previous Friday (18th May).

John must therefore post his cheque by 15th June rather than 16th June to ensure it reaches HMRC on time.

If the cheque arrived on Saturday 19th May, it would be treated by HMRC as having been received on Monday 21 May and the payment would be regarded as late.

If John paid late on one more occasion during 2012/13, he would suffer a late payment penalty.

This can be avoided by posting the cheque a few days early when the normal payment date falls on a weekend.

32. Dispensations For Employers

You can save a considerable amount of time and money by applying to HMRC for a dispensation for certain business expenses reimbursed to employees by the company.

A dispensation frees the employer from having to report certain expenses to HMRC and can be granted for those expenses in respect of which a corresponding tax deduction can be claimed.

A dispensation also removes the need for the employee to claim the tax deduction, saving work all round.

This applies to any size of company, from a one-person company to large multi-nationals, although obviously the more employees you have, the more time you will save in not having to complete the sections of the P11D that are no longer relevant once a dispensation has been granted.

Dispensations for Employers

John is fed up with the time-consuming job of completing P11Ds for his employees when all he does is reimburse business expenses.

He applies for and is granted a dispensation for the business expenses of his employees.

This means that he no longer has to complete P11Ds for the employees as no benefits are reportable. Therefore it leaves him with more time to get on with running the business.

33. Claim A Deduction For Mileage Payments

Under the Approved Mileage Allowance Payments (AMAP) Scheme employers can pay employees tax-free mileage rates when they use their own car for business. Provided that the amounts paid do not exceed the rates set by HMRC, no tax liability arises and there is nothing to report on the P11D.

However, many employees are unaware that if their employer pays them at a rate that is less than the approved rate they can claim a tax deduction for the shortfall. The approved rates for 2012/13 for cars and vans are 45p per mile for the first 10,000 business miles in the tax year and 25p thereafter.

Claim a Deduction for Mileage Allowances

John uses his own car for work and in 2012/13 undertakes 9,000 business miles. His employer pays a mileage allowance of 35p per mile. Thus John receives mileage allowances of £2,700 during the year.

However, at the approved rate of 45p per mile for the first 10,000 business miles, John's employer could pay him a tax-free allowance of £4,050 (9,000 miles @ 45p per mile). This is known as the approved amount.

John can claim a tax deduction of£1,350 for the shortfall between the approved amount (£4,050) and the amount he is actually paid (£2,700). Assuming John is a higher rate tax payer paying tax at 40%, this will save him tax of £540.

34. Capital Allowances: Annual Investment Allowance

Ensuring that the annual investment allowance is claimed on all new items of plant and machinery can save considerable amounts of tax.

The annual investment allowance gives a 100% deduction against profits up to the amount of the allowance. The allowance is £25,000 from 1 April 2012 (corporation tax) and 6 April 2012 (income tax).

Capital Allowances: Annual Investment Allowance

John buys £10,000 worth of equipment for his small business.

He claims the annual investment allowance, which reduces his taxable profit for the year by £10,000.

If John pays tax at the small profits rate of 20%, this will save him £2,000 a year. If the business in unincorporated, the saving will be at his marginal rate of tax.

If as an alternative, he chooses not to claim the annual investment allowance, he can instead claim the normal 18% writing down allowance and have a deduction from his taxable profit of £1,800.

In certain circumstances it can be more beneficial to claim the writing down allowance rather than the annual investment allowance.

This may be the case where the capital allowance is increasing a loss that is eating into a personal allowance rather than generating a tax rebate.

Claiming the writing down allowance may also be preferable if the intention is to dispose of the asset after a short period of time so as to minimise balancing charges on the disposal.

35.   Short Life Assets

Capital items with an expected lifespan of less than five years can be treated as short life assets by making a relevant claim.

This means the asset is not added to the general capital allowances pool and if disposed of within the five years then the loss on scrapping or sale will be realised straight away rather than affecting the general pool.

If the asset is still held after five years then it is automatically added back into the general pool.

Short Life Assets

John buys £10,000 worth of new equipment which he thinks will last less than five years, and hence elects to treat these as short life assets.

After three years he is proved right when the equipment has passed its useful life and is scrapped, at which point he can claim a balancing allowance for the remainder of his original cost against his profits.

---

36. Choose A Low Emission Car And Claim 100% First Year Capital Allowances

The annual investment allowance is not available in respect of cars. However, it is still possible to obtain a 100% deduction against profits for a car purchased for your business by choosing a car with very low CO_2 emissions (110 g/km or less). To qualify, the car must be purchased on or before 31 March 2013.

Make sure you keep all receipts for expenses incurred in this way.

Choose a low emission car and claim 100% first-year capital allowances

John has a small family business and is looking to buy a company car.

He chooses a car that has CO_2 emissions of 105 g/km and which cost £15,000.

As the car's CO_2 emissions are less than 110 g/km he can claim a 100% first-year allowance thereby obtaining an immediate write-off against profits of £15,000.

If he pays tax at the small profits rate of 20% (financial year 2012) claiming the 100% FYA rather than an 18% WDA will save tax of £2,460 in that year. However, if he delays the purchase to beyond 3 March 2013, he will not benefit from the 100% first-year allowance and will instead only qualify for the WDA.

Choosing a low emission car also minimises the benefit in kind tax that John will pay on the company car.

37.   Claim Your Pre-Trading Expenditure

Many people are not aware that you can claim expenses incurred in the seven years before commencement of trading against your first year's trading profits.

The expenses are treated as having been occurred on the first day of trading. The same rules apply to determine whether a pre-trading expense is deductible as apply normally for determining deductibility of expenses.

Make sure you keep all receipts for expenses incurred in this way.

Claim for Pre-Trading Expenditure

John has incurred pre-trading expenses of over £5,000 and has kept all his receipts for these expenses, which are all qualifying expenses.

As a result, his profit in his first year of self-employment is lowered by £5,000. A 50% taxpayer would save £2,500 in tax, a 40% taxpayer, £2,000 in tax and a basic rate taxpayer £1,000 in tax.

So once again, make sure you keep all those receipts as you could make a very significant tax saving.

---

38. Complete The Short Self-Employment Pages If Your Turnover Is Below £70,000

If your self-employment turnover is less than £70,000per annum then there is no need to go to the trouble and expense of completing the full Self-Employment Supplementary pages (SA103F)and detailing all your expenses.

Instead you can complete the short Self-Employment Supplementary pages (SA103S; see www.hmrc.gov.uk/forms/sa103s.pdf), which is only two pages long and save time by entering total expenses in box 19 rather than providing details of specific expenses..

Self Employed with turnover of less than £70,000

Bill sets up in self-employment and commences to trade on 6 April 2011.

His total turnover is £20,000 to 31 March 2012 and hence he can save time and money by only completing the short self-employment pages (SA103S).

39. Submit Your Tax Return Online

By submitting your Tax Return Online you have longer to do it.

Returns submitted in paper format must reach HMRC by 31 October after the end of the tax year.

However, if you file your return online you have until the following 31 January to do it.

A penalty is charged if your return is submitted late. If you file a paper return after 31 October the penalty applies. Under the new penalty structure, the later the return is filed, the higher the penalty charged.

However, if you miss the paper filing date and file online instead by 31 January you will save yourself the penalty.

Filing online also has the added benefit that your tax is worked out automatically.

To find out more about filing your Tax Return online, visit the HMRC website (www.hmrc.gov.uk).

40. File Your Tax Return By 30 December

Although you have until 31 January after the end of the tax year to file your Tax Return, if you file it online by 30 December and the amount of tax that you owe is less than £3,000, you can have the tax you owe collected through your PAYE code, rather than having to pay it in one go by 31 January.

This has considerable cashflow advantages.

File Your Tax Return by 30 December

John files his Tax Return online on 15 December. He pays tax at 40%. He owes tax of £1,800 and chooses to have the tax collected through his PAYE code. This delays payment and saves him from having to make a payment of £720.

---

41.   Use Rounding In Your Tax Return

If you have income that includes 'pence', round down these figures.

For expenses always round them up.

Multiple figures for one entry cannot be rounded until the final figure is calculated, at which point this figure can be rounded up or down as appropriate.

This may not save you a lot of tax but every little bit helps!

Use Rounding in Your Tax Return

John is self-employed and uses 15 boxes on his Return in total.

By rounding, he may save tax on up to £14.85, or £5.94 in tax for a 40% taxpayer.

---

42.   Avoid Unnecessary Interest

By ensuring that you pay any tax on time, you can avoid paying the HMRC non-deductible interest for the late payment of tax.

Avoid Unnecessary Interest

John files his Tax Return in March, and discovers that he has a liability of £100 for the year, which he paid on 16 March.

Because he paid his tax late, he is liable for:

- interest on the late paid tax,

- a further 5% surcharge because the tax was still unpaid on 28 February

He could quite easily have avoided the interest charge by paying his tax on time.

---

43. File Your Tax Return On Time To Avoid Hefty Penalties

Hefty penalties apply to people who fail to file their tax return on time. New tougher penalties now apply which mean that you could pay as much as £1,300 in penalties if you file your tax return six months late.

The longer the delay in filing the return, the higher the penalty is charged. Paper returns for 2011/12 must be filed by 31 October 2012 and online returns must be filed by 31 January 2013.

Where a return if filed after these dates, a penalty is charged.

The penalty is £100 if the return is filed one day late. If the return is filed up to three months late, a further penalty of £10 per day is charged to a maximum of £900. If the return is filed six months late a further penalty of £300 or 5% of the tax due, if higher, is charged.

A further penalty of £300 or 5% of the tax due, if higher, is charged if the return is still outstanding after 12 months.

File your tax return on time to avoid hefty new penalties

John files his 2011/12 self-assessment return online in August 2013 The return was due by 31 January 2013. The tax due was £1,000. The return was filed more than six months late and John is charged a penalty of £1,300. This could easily have been avoided had John been more organised and filed his return by the deadline of 31 January 2012.

The penalties apply in addition to interest and surcharges on late-paid tax.

44.   Do You Need A Tax Return?

You can save yourself a considerable amount of time, effort and expense if you employ a tax adviser by finding out whether you still need to complete a Return after changes in your circumstances.

HMRC are keen to reduce their workload in processing self-assessment returns where they are no longer required and you should review this after any change of circumstances.

Visit the HMRC website at www.hmrc.gov.uk/sa/need-tax-return.htm#1 to see if you need to complete a Tax Return.

Do You Need a Tax Return?

John was self-employed for a few years, but has been an employee on PAYE earning under £30,000 per annum for the past two years.

He has no other sources of income or gains.

As he is sent a Tax Return each year, his accountant duly files this and charges a fee for determining that no tax is due.

By checking with HMRC whether he still needs to file and receiving a response that he is being removed from the obligation to file, he saves himself the time and expense of having to complete the form each year.

---

45. Registering Your Capital Losses

If you bought an asset and sold it at a loss then it is possible that you made a capital loss (e.g. if you traded internet/technology shares during the technology bubble or brought an investment property that went down in value, then this may well apply to you).

In order to preserve this loss for use against gains in future years, you must return the loss within your Tax Return within six years, or amend an already filed Return to claim the loss. Alternatively a claim can be made by writing to the tax inspector.

Note that if gains were incurred during the year that the loss was made, the loss will first be set against the other gains for the year before being carried forward.

This is regardless of whether the gains are below the annual CGT exemption (£10,600 for the 2012/13 tax year).

Remember, any size loss if realised in isolation can be used in this way, and could save you 28% tax on the amount of the loss in future years.

Therefore always claim losses in the year in which they arise and keep a note of the amount of losses you have accumulated.

Registering Your Capital Losses

John sold some shares realising a significant loss of £20,000 in 2008, and had no other disposals in the year.

He is now selling his investment property on which he will realise a significant capital gain. The sale takes place in 2012/13.

In order to utilise the loss, he submits a revised Tax Return for 2008 showing the capital loss, which is accepted by HMRC. The loss is carried forward to future years.

He can now use the loss against his capital gain in 2012/13 which saves £5,600 in tax (£20,000 @28%).

46. Make A Claim Negligible Value Claim For Worthless Assets

If you own an asset that has become worthless you can make a claim to treat the asset as if you had sold the asset and immediately required it at the time of the claim for it value at that time.

The claim, known as a negligible value claim enables relief to be given for the loss in value of the asset.

The loss is treated as arising in the year in which the claim is made, or at a time specified in the claim in the two preceding tax years during at which time the conditions for the claim were met.

> **Make a negligible value claim for worthless assets**
>
> John subscribed for shares in a company. The shares cost £10,000 in 2005. The company failed in October 2012 and the shares became worthless.
>
> John makes a negligible value claim for 2012/13 for the loss on the shares of £10,000. The loss can be set against capital gains. Alternatively, it can be set against his income of 2012/13 or 2011/12 if he has no gains for 2012/13 and does not want to carry the loss forward to set against future capital gains.
>
> Assuming John is a higher rate taxpayer, the claim will save tax of £2,800 if the loss is offset against capital gains and tax of £4,000 if set against income.

47.   Registering Your Rental Losses

If you rent out property then you have an obligation to report the property income and expenses to HMRC, even if you make a loss.

Many people do not realise this and only start reporting the income when they break into profit.

Without reporting the rental losses, you are losing out on being able to set these losses against future income from property, meaning that you will pay more tax than you should.

So if you register these losses now then you will be able to take them forward and offset them in future years.

Registering your Rental Losses

John starts letting out a property in 2005.

For each of the first five years, he calculates a loss of £1,000 per annum and declares this loss on his Tax Return.

Due to changes in mortgage rates and a rise in rental income from the property, he realises a profit of £2,500 in each of the years2011 and 2012, which he also declares.

Because he has declared the losses in the previous five years, he utilises the losses against the income and saves tax on this income.

Assuming John pays tax at 40%, the saving by using the losses is £2,000.

---

48.   Utilise Rent A Room Relief

If you rent out a room within your own property then you can claim the rent a room relief of £4,250.

This can be claimed against the rental income as an alternative to claiming the expenses incurred in letting the room out.

In many cases this eliminates the tax charge entirely, just for ticking a box on the Tax Return form.

It is worth comparing actual costs against this relief to determine whether or not it is more worthwhile claiming the relief rather than the expenses - this will be dependent on the level of expenses compared to the relief, even where the total rental income exceeds the £4,250 threshold.

Where there are two or more sharers renting out rooms, each can claim relief of £2,125. This means that it is possible to earn tax-free rental income under the rent-a-room scheme of more than £4,250 in respect of one property.

Rent a Room Relief

Scenario 1 – When it is beneficial to use the relief

John rents out a room in his house for £4,250 per annum, incurring very little in the way of costs, and pays tax on £3,000 of this income at 40%.

He is unaware of rent a room relief until he appoints a tax consultant to deal with his tax affairs, and claims it for 2012/13. By making the claim, he saves paying the tax on the £3,000 which is £1,200.

Scenario 2 – When it is not beneficial to use the relief

John rents out a room and, after expenses, makes a loss of £1,000 as the rental income is £6,000 and his expenses £7,000.

Clearly here he is better off not making the election, as to do so would turn his £1,000 loss into a profit of £1,750 on which he would incur tax, as under the rent-a-room where income exceeds the £4,250 limit the excess over the limit is taxed.

49.   Furnished Holiday Lettings

From 6 April 2011, the rules on using losses from furnished holiday lettings became stricter so that it is now only possible to set the losses arising from a furnished holiday lettings business against profits from same furnished holiday lettings business, It is no longer possible to set losses against general income.

As all UK furnished holiday lets by the same person are treated as part of the same FHL business, losses on one property are effectively offset against profits from other properties in the same year. Losses are not restricted to set off against the same property, just the same FHL business.

However, under the revised rules, furnished holiday letting are still treated as a trade and retain some of the advantages.

Capital allowances may be claimed in respect of plant and machinery. Capital gains tax reliefs, such as entrepreneurs' relief and rollover relief may also be available.

However, to qualify as a furnished holiday letting and to benefit from associated advantages, the minimum period for which the property must be let is to increase from 70 days to 105 days per year from 2012/13 and the period for which it must be available for letting is to increase from 140 to 210 days from the same date.

To continue to benefit from the FHL rules, steps must be taken to ensure that these new conditions are met.

However, a period of grace is allowed such that if a property ceases to meet the FHL letting conditions to remain within the regime for one or two years on making a claim. This is worthwhile as allows time to increase the letting without having to deal with the consequences of becoming a non-holiday let (such as possible balancing charges).

Where a property is let on short term lets, the FHL rules offer advantages over other lets and it is still worthwhile to fall within the FHL regime, despite the restriction on loss relief.

Furnished Holiday Lettings

John buys a house in Brighton, which qualifies as a furnished holiday letting.

He makes a loss in the 2012/13 of £5,000, which he can set against future income from his FHL business.

After three years, he sells the property.

He is able to benefit from the capital gains tax reliefs available for traders, such as rollover relief and entrepreneur's relief.

---

50. Claim Your 10% Wear And Tear Allowance

If you let a property furnished, not only does the property normally generate more income, but you can claim the 10% wear and tear deduction from the gross rentals received.

Many non-represented taxpayers regularly miss out on this very easy relief.

Claim Your 10% Wear & Tear Allowance

John buys an investment property and discusses the merits and downsides of letting the property furnished or unfurnished with his tax adviser.

By letting it furnished he obtains a deduction from his gross rents of £2,000 per annum.

If he pays tax at 40%, this saves £800 in tax annually.

---

51.   Use The Gift Aid Scheme

By making sure you fill in a gift aid scheme form when giving money to charity, the charity can recover the tax on this payment, boosting your contribution to them by 20% of the grossed up amount. The charity can reclaim 25% of the net donation.

Higher rate taxpayers qualify for higher rate tax relief on such payments, resulting in a refund of 20% for higher rate taxpayers paying tax at 40% and a refund of 30% for additional rate taxpayers paying tax at 50%. For additional rate taxpayers, the refund will drop to 25% from 5 April 2013 as a result of the fall in the additional rate to 45% from that date. Additional rate taxpayers may wish to make large donations before 6 April 2013 to take advantage of relief at 50%.

Check to ensure you claim this relief if you are a higher or additional rate taxpayer and make a gift aid payment, no matter how small.

Many attractions offer the chance to make such donations using the scheme, so get a receipt showing the amount of the donation and claim back your tax.

Use the Gift Aid Scheme

John makes Gift Aid donations of £800 during the year, on which the charities concerned recover 20% tax on the grossed up amount.

John pays tax at the higher rate of 40%. The gross donation of £1,000 can be included in his Tax Return resulting in a refund to him of £200.

52.   Principal Private Residence Relief (PPR)

There are many rules associated with this relief, but remember to make use of this exemption as for the majority of people this is the biggest investment they ever make.

Where you own more than one home you can choose which one is your main residence as long as both have been lived in as your main residence at some point. By making the appropriate election it is possible to maximise the benefit of the relief. Professional advice should be sought prior to making an election.

Principal Private Residence (PPR)

John sells his house in 2012 for £450,000, having purchased the property in 2004 for £375,000. As it is his PPR, no tax is payable on the gain he has made on this property.

---

53. Private Lettings Relief

If you rent out a property, which was at one time your PPR, you will qualify for the lettings relief.

This can be worth up to £40,000 against the gain realised on the disposal of a property.

Note that this relief is per person, so if property is held jointly it can attract up to £80,000 relief.

Unrepresented taxpayers frequently miss this relief from their calculation of the chargeable gain on a property where they can have claimed it.

Private Lettings Relief

John and Mary sell their investment property, which at one time used to be their main home.

They qualify for the maximum relief and save paying tax on £80,000 of the gain. Where capital gains tax is payable at the higher rate of 28%, this results in a tax saving of £22,400.

54. The 36 Month Rule

If a property was once at some point your PPR then the last 36 months are exempt from tax.

This means that if you have a second property that you now live in, then you are still entitled to PPR for the last 36 months on the other property.

The 36 Month Rule

John sells a property he has been renting out for the last 8 years. He actually owned it for 10 years as he lived in it for the first two years.

When the property is sold he realises a profit of £100,000 before PPR relief.

His actual PPR relief would be 2/10ths of the gain (i.e. the first two years he lived in it), but by using the 36 month rule a further 3/10ths of the gain drops out of charge, leaving him with a gain of £50,000 instead of £80,000.

This provides a tax saving on some £30,000 of gain, or £8,400 in capital gains tax at 28%.

In addition, John qualifies for the lettings exemption, further reducing his gain.

55.   Choosing Your PPR

Where you have more than one property it is possible to choose which one is your PPR at any given time, provided the property is or has been used as a home. This option is available to everyone – not just MPs. However, a person can only have on PPR at any one time.

By `flipping' the properties, it is possible to maximise relied and ensure that the last 36 months for each PPR qualify for relief.

Choosing your PPR

John has a flat in the city that he bought for £100,000 in April 2000. In April 2003 he buys a family home in the country for £400,000.

He elects for the country home to be his PPR.

He sells the country home in July 2011 for £700,000, buying a larger property nearby. As the property has been his PPR throughout the gain is tax-free.

He also sells the flat in July 2011 to fund the larger property, making a gain of £150,000. He is able to claim PPR in respect of the periods from April 2000 to April 2003 and also for the last 36 months.

Had John not flipped his properties so that his country home was his PPR, he would not have been entitled to PPR on the sale and the gain of £300,000 would have attracted capital gains tax.

Although some of the gain on the flat is taxable, the overall tax bill is much reduced.

---

56. Check Your Tax Code

Your tax code determines how much tax is deducted under PAYE, You should always check your tax code is correct as errors may result in too much or too little tax being deducted.

HMRC may also adjust the code to collect tax on savings income. You do not need to have this collected through your code.

Instead you can ask HMRC to take it the savings adjustment out of your code and pay the tax under the self-assessment system. This will increase your take home pay each month.

Where an individual's income is over £100,000 the personal allowance is reduced by £1 for every £2 of income above £100,000.

Where HMRC expect the allowance to be abated on the basis that the previous year's income was in excess of £100,000, they will take away the personal allowance from the tax code.

If your income is likely to be less than £100,000 you can ask that they readjust the code, rather than waiting until you do your Tax Return to claim a repayment.

This will provide a cash flow advantage.

Check Your Tax Code

John has a company car.

In April 2012 he changed his car to a more environmentally friendly model.

As replacement cars do not now need to be notified to HMRC on form P46 (Car) (although employers can provide HMRC with this information online if they want to), HMRC may not be aware of the change until his P11D for 2012/13 is submitted in July 2013.

John's tax code for 2012/13 is based on his previous car and consequently John pays more tax than he needs to each month as a result.

By checking his tax code and telling HMRC about the change, he will have more take home pay each month.

57.   Payments On Account

If your total net tax liability for the year is less than £1,000, or if at least 80% of the total tax due for the year is covered by tax deducted at source, then you do not need to make payments on account for the following tax year.

The second test is sometimes missed by HMRC and people are asked to make payments on account unnecessarily, resulting in a loss of the use of the money unnecessarily early.

Payments on Account

John calculates his tax liability at £7,000 for the year2011/12, of which £1,200 relates to investment income payable under self-assessment. The remainder (£5,800) was deducted under PAYE.

Because his tax liability is over the £1,000 limit, he assumes he has to make payments on account for the following year and hence enters these figures onto his Tax Return.

However, as over 80% of his total tax liability is deducted at source under PAYE, he meets the second test and does not need to make payments on account. The tax on his investment income is payable in full by 31 January of the end of the tax year. By being aware of this test, he avoids making payments on account and benefits from the associated cash flow advantage.

---

58. Check HMRC's Computation

If you submit your own Tax Return online or even if you submit a paper return before 31 October and ask HMRC to do the calculation for you, always check HMRC's calculation for obvious errors, as sometimes computations can be incorrect.

If you don't check the computation then HMRC will ask you for the tax calculated.

This could potentially result in paying much more tax than is properly due.

Check HMRC's Computation

John submits his Tax Return in paper format before 31 October and asks HMRC to calculate the tax for him.

His own calculation shows that he is due to pay £500 this year, but HMRC's calculation comes back and shows a liability of £1,000 due to an error by HMRC.

He assumes he has made a mistake and ends up paying too much tax.

This could be easily avoided by checking the computation or having the Tax Return professionally prepared together with a tax calculation, so that your tax adviser can query any mistakes by HMRC and get them rectified.

---

59. Watch Out For the Online Tax Calculation...

Where the tax return is submitted online, the associated tax calculation shows the tax due for the year, not the balance which needs to be paid.

Where payments on account have been made during the year, these need to be deducted from the liability for the year to show the balance due if any for the year of the return.

It is only this balance, plus the first payment on account for the following year that needs to be paid by 31 January after the end of the tax year.

Watch Out For the Online Tax Calculation

John files his 2011/12 tax return online in December 2012.

The tax return calculation shows that his liability for the year is £4,500 and that his payments on account for 2012/13 are £2,250 on each of 31 January 2013 and 31 July 2013.

John assumes this means that he must pay tax of £6,750 (liability of £4,500 plus first payment on account of £2,250) by 31 January 2013, which he pays.

However, this calculation does not reflect the payments of account in respect of the 2011/12 liability of £2,000 made in January 2012 and of £2,000 in July 2012 (a total of £4000).

As a result, John should have only paid a balancing payment of £500 for 2011/12 and the first payment on account for 2012/13 by 31 January 2013 (a total of £2,750)

He will have overpaid tax of £4,000 and will doubtless have to wait for this to be refunded by HMRC. Not good from a cashflow perspective.

60. National Savings Certificates

National savings certificates pay interest tax free and it is currently possible to invest up to £15,000 per issue in these and receive tax free interest. The minimum investment is £100. This can save quite a bit of tax. Although tax-effective for all taxpayers, they are particularly tax efficient for those paying tax at the higher or additional rates.

There are two types of tax-free savings certificates – indexed-linked certificates (which provide inflation-beating returns) and fixed-interest certificates (which provide a guaranteed return).

The 48th issue of Index Linked Savings Certificates was launched in May 2011 and provides a guaranteed compound rate of annual equivalent rate (AER) of interest over 5 years of index linking plus 0.50%. Savings certificates are linked to the retail prices index, which provides the highest measure of inflation. Although they are designed to be held for five years, they can be cashed in early making them a good short-term investment. However, no index-linking or interest is paid if they are cashed within the first year. They can also be taken out by anyone over the age of seven, making them a suitable investment by or on behalf of children.

The rates on these products vary from time to time but are reasonably competitive taking into account their tax free status.

National Savings Certificates

John invests £60,000 into National Savings Certificates and receives a yield of 2.75%. This is equivalent to £1,650 in interest.

By holding his savings in this way, he saves having to pay tax on this income, which at a tax rate of 40% is a saving of £660 a year.

---

61. Children's Bonus Bond

Children's bonus bonds are another tax free investment issued by National Savings.

Children bonus bonds allow investments to be made in the child's own name and there is no tax to pay on the interest or on any bonuses. The maximum investment per issue is £3,000 per issue (minimum £25 per issue) and the term is a minimum of five years.

This can be a useful product for generating income and a nest egg for your children and is not affected by the rules concerning income generated by gifts from parents for children.

For issue 34, each £25 unit earns an interest rate of 2.50% AER including the five year bonus.

Children's Bonus Bond

John invests £3,000 into a Children's Bonus Bond to be held for the benefit of his one-year-old daughter Kelly.

By holding it in this bond, he saves tax on the interest income as he has used up the £100 limit already on other savings in her name.

62. Do You Have Savings And Are Still Paying A Mortgage?

If the interest rate on your mortgage is higher than the interest you earn on your savings, then you can save a considerable amount of money and reduce your tax bill on interest received, by using spare capital to pay off the mortgage on your own property. In the current climate of low interest rates where savings earn a very poor rate of return this is likely to be worthwhile.

You could also save considerable tax by switching to an offset mortgage if you feel the need to have the capital easily available should the need for it arise.

Remember that your mortgage payments are made from your after-tax income and hence cost you a lot more in total income to fund than you may think.

Savings and Mortgages

John has £30,000 earning 2% per annum in interest, which equates to 1.2% net of higher rate tax at 40%. He also has a mortgage of £30,000 on which he pays interest at a rate of 3.5% on his mortgage. This costs him £1,050 a year, which is payable from his after tax income.

By paying off the mortgage, he no longer pays the £1,050 in interest per annum on this and also no longer receives the £373 in interest the money earned him after tax. He is therefore £677 a year better off.

To fund the mortgage payments was costing John £1,750 in gross income, which he could now use for other purposes i.e. increase his pension funding, which would save him further tax.

63.   Pension Funding By Companies

A payment within the limits into a pension scheme for a director is a tax-deductible item for the company and is not classed as a benefit for the director. Contributions by a company on behalf of a director or employee count towards the annual allowance limit on tax-relieved pension contributions.

Therefore this can be a useful way of extracting surplus funds from a company or avoiding higher rate tax on further dividends or salary payments where the funds are not required to live on and surplus cash is building up within the company.

Note –special rules apply to spread pension contributions if these are excessively high in a particular year.

Pension Funding by Companies

John pays himself a salary of £35,000 per annum from the company, and is aged 30.

He does not need any more income than this, and any additional salary or dividend will attract tax at the higher rate in his hands.

The company can pay a large contribution into a personal pension scheme on his behalf and no tax is payable on this contribution.

The contribution is tax deductible when computing the profits of the company and therefore saves corporation tax. For the financial year 2012 the small profits rate of corporation tax is 20% and the main rate is 24%.

64. Self-Employed? Then Consider Incorporation

Although the basic rate of income tax at 20% is the same as the small profits rate of corporation tax (20% in financial year 2012), it can still be beneficial to incorporate and extract funds by way of dividends.

This is because dividends do not attract National Insurance contributions so by incorporating you will save Class 4 National Insurance contributions.

The rise in National Insurance contributions from 6 April 2011 (main rate Class 4 contributions increased from 8% to 9% and additional rate contributions from 1% to 2% from this date) increased the savings from incorporating and paying dividends.

Self-employed and Incorporation

John incorporates on 6 April 2012, and makes a profit of £50,000 in his first year.

Not only does he now have a choice as to whether to draw this income and pay personal taxes on it or leave it in the company and only incur corporation tax on this, but he also saves a considerable amount of tax by paying himself in dividends rather than a salary as these do not attract National Insurance Contributions.

65. Pay A Small Salary To Retain Entitlement To The State Pension

Where a person's earnings fall between the lower earnings limit for Class 1 National Insurance purposes (£107 per week for 2012/13) and the primary earnings threshold (£46 per week for2012/13) they are deemed to have paid National Insurance contributions at a notional zero rate.

The benefit of this is that it preserves their contribution record and entitlement to the state pension and certain contributory benefits, without actually costing them anything.

Therefore where profits are extracted in the form of dividends, it is beneficial to also pay a small salary.

For2012/13, although the salary can be between £5,564 and £7,605 for the year (£464 to £634 per month) to enjoy the benefit of 'free' employee contributions, as the secondary threshold at £144 per week (the level at which employer contributions start) is lower than the primary threshold (£146 per week), a salary of between £5,564 and £7,488 per annum (£464 and £624 per month) will achieve this aim without triggering an employer Class 1 liability.

As a salary at this level is below the PAYE threshold, no PAYE tax needs to be paid.

Earnings and the Entitlement to State Retirement Pension

John employs his wife, sister, brother and two siblings in the family business on a part time basis, paying each of them £575 per month (£6,900 a year).

None of them have any other sources of income and the salaries are fully justifiable commercially.

The payments also meet National Minimum Wage requirements.

By paying these salaries he is cutting his own tax bill (by paying his family members instead of himself) and they are accruing entitlement to state pension and other benefits without actually paying any tax or National Insurance contributions.

66. Keeping Entitlement to Child Benefit

Proposals to take-away child benefit from higher rate earners provoked something of a political storm and led to the Chancellor watering down the original proposals.

As announced in the March 2012 Budget, from 7 January 2013 a new child benefit income tax charge will apply where either a person in receipt of child benefit or his or her live in partner (whether or not they are married or in a civil partnership) has income of £50,000 or more.

The charge is set at 1% of the child benefit awarded for each £100 where income exceeds £50,000. Where income is £60,000 or more, the charge will equal the child benefit paid in the year.

Where the recipient does not live with a partner and has income of £50,000 or more a year, it is the recipient who will pay the charge. However, where a couple live together, if one only one person has income in excess of £50,000 that person will pay the charge. Where both parties have income in excess of £50,000 the person with the higher income will pay the charge. This means the person paying the income tax charge will not necessarily be the same person who receives the benefit.

It is possible for a couple each earning £49,999 (a total income of £99,998) to retain full child benefit, whereas a single person with an income of £60,000 will have all his or her child benefit clawed back.

Where one partner has income of more than £50,000, redistributing income may enable the couple to retain their child benefit. Similarly, in a single parent household where income exceeds £50,000, reducing income to below £50,000 by, say, delaying payments, entering into a salary sacrifice or contributing to a pension, may allow child benefit to be retained in full. Keeping income below £60,000 if it is not possible to reduce income to below £50,000 will mean at least not all child benefit is clawed back.

Keeping entitlement to child benefit

Henry and Paula both work in the family business. They have two children and receive child benefit of £1,752 a year (2012/13 rates)

Henry earns £65,000 and Paula earns £25,000. The child benefit is paid to Paula. However, as Henry's income is above £60,000, from 7 January 2013 he will suffer an income tax charge equal to the full amount of the child benefit paid to Paula.

By reducing the income paid to Henry to £45,000 and increasing the income paid to Paula to £45,000, the child benefit charge does not apply and they are able to keep the full amount of their child benefit. At current rates this will make them £1,752 a year better off, despite the fact that their combined income is unchanged.

67. Keeping Entitlement To Statutory Sick Pay And Other Statutory Payments

Entitlement to statutory sick pay, statutory maternity pay, statutory paternity pay and statutory adoption pay is dependent on average weekly earnings for the required period being at least equal to the lower earnings limit for National Insurance purposes (£107 per week for2012/13).

As seen above, paying a small salary of around £7,000 a year will preserve entitlement to the state pension. It will also ensure that an employee is entitled to statutory sick pay and also, where relevant, statutory maternity pay, statutory paternity pay and statutory adoption pay.

68. Paying A Bonus To Increase SMP

Statutory maternity pay is paid at a rate of 90% of average weekly earnings for the first six weeks and at the standard rate (£135.45 for2012/13) for the remainder (or 90% of average weekly earnings if less).

Paying a bonus in the period over which average weekly earnings are calculated will increase the employee's average weekly earnings and therefore the SMP payable in the first six weeks.

Small employers (total annual NIC bill of £45,000 or less) can recover 103% (2012/13 rate) of any SMP paid, so the additional SMP paid to the employee does not cost the employer extra.

Paying a Bonus to Increase SMP

John has his own company and employs his daughter Jayne. She is expecting her first baby. Her average weekly earnings, based on her normal salary, are £500 per week. She is due a bonus of £2,400.

By paying her the bonus during the set period, the bonus is taken into account in calculating her average weekly earnings.

As a result her average weekly earnings are increased to £800 per week. This increases the SMP payable in the first six weeks of her maternity leave from £450 per week (90% of £500) to £720 per week (90% of £800).

John can reclaim the SMP paid so the extra SMP costs him nothing.

---

69.   Children And Gifts Of Capital

Although income from gifts from parents is treated as that of the parents if it exceeds £100 per annum, gifts from other relatives do not suffer this treatment.

Therefore to save some tax and utilise your children's personal allowances, ask your relatives to gift your children money and you can do likewise for their children (although ensure there is not a connection between one gift and another).

> **Children and Gifts of Capital**
>
> John's mother gifts his children £3,000 per annum to utilise her IHT exemption.
>
> The income generated by this gift is covered by the children's personal allowances, and hence tax is saved as a result.

70. Losses And Tax Credits

If you are self-employed and usually make large profits, but incurred a loss for one year, then you may be eligible to claim working families' tax credits for that year.

It is worth submitting a protective claim during any year for which you are uncertain of the level of your income as you can only backdate claims for three months from the date of claim.

Losses and Tax Credits

John is married to Mary, who does not work. They have one child age 10.

John usually makes £100,000 per annum as a self-employed consultant.

However, he has just lost his major customer and as a result is likely to make a loss this year, and so submits a claim to working families' tax credits. It turns out he does make a loss, and receives over £1,000 in tax credits.

71. Small Earnings Exemption For Class 2 NIC

If you earn less than £5,595 (2012/13 figures) a year from your self-employment you are entitled to claim the small earnings exemption and not pay any Class 2 NIC for the year.

At £2.65 a week this is a yearly saving of £137.80 in National Insurance.

Remember that you can also claim this for any year in which you have a loss.

Small Earnings Exemption for Class 2 NIC

Mark has a small self-employment business as well as his full time employment.

He earns £20,000 in his employment and £4,000 from his self-employment.

Because his self-employment earnings are below the small earnings limit for Class 2 NIC, he can claim exemption and save himself Class 2 contributions of £2.65 a week (2012/13 figures).

72. Deferring National Insurance Contributions

National Insurance contributions are worked out separately for each employment and self-employment, without taking account of any other earnings on which NICs are payable.

This means that where a person has more than one job or has income from both employment and self-employment, they may end up paying National Insurance contributions in excess of the annual maximum for the year.

Where it looks likely contributions will be paid in excess of the annual maximum, contributions can be deferred. An application for deferment for Class 1 contributions is made on form CA72A (see www.hmrc.gov.uk/forms/ca72a-2010-11pdf). And an application to defer Class 2 and/or Class 4 contributions is made on form CA72B (www.hmrc.gov.uk/forms/ca72b.pdf).

73.   The 10% Savings Rate Of Tax

Savings income is charged to tax at a rate of 10% up to the savings rate limit of £2,710 (2012/13 figures). The savings rate only applies if taxable non-savings income does not exceed the savings rate limit.

If you have savings income that qualifies for the savings rate and that income has suffered a tax deduction of source at 20% (for example bank interest paid net), you can reclaim the difference between the tax deducted (20%) and the tax due at the savings rate (10%) on form R40.

You can download the form via the following link: http://www.hmrc.gov.uk/forms/r40.pdf.

The 10% Savings Rate of Tax

John receives bank interest of £8,000 (net). The interest has suffered deduction of tax at the basic rate of 20%. This is John's only income.

John has gross savings income of £10,000 (£8,000 x 100/80). He is entitled to the personal allowance of £8,105 for 2012/13. His taxable savings income is therefore £1,895. As this is less than the savings rate limit for 2012/13 of £2,710, John pays tax at the savings rate of 10%.

The tax due on John's savings is therefore £189.50 (£1,895 @ 10%).

He has suffered tax at source of £2,000.

He can therefore reclaim £1,810.50 on form R40. The claim extends not only to the savings income covered by his personal allowance (£1,621 being £8,105 @20%), but also repayment of half the tax suffered at source on his taxable savings income of £1,895 (£189.50), which is liable to tax at 10% rather than the 20% deducted.

74.   Unlisted Share Losses

Many people subscribe for shares in unlisted companies. These can include companies that your friends own.

A number of these companies will fail and therefore the original investment is lost.

Allowable losses on these shares can be set against income rather than used as a capital loss, which is especially useful if you have no other gains during the year or are unlikely to make capital gains in the future.

> **Unlisted Share Losses**
>
> Louise subscribed for 1000 shares in ABC Ltd. a company set up by her brother, and paid £10,000 for them. They are now worthless as the company has closed down. She pays tax at 40%. By claiming income tax relief on this capital loss, she recovers £4,000 of the loss. Had she claimed relief as a capital loss, she would only have recovered £2,800 of the loss.

75.   Interest Relief

By restructuring your borrowings, it may be possible to obtain higher or additional rate tax relief on your borrowings.

Tax relief is available for borrowing to fund a buy-to-let property to the value of the property when first met. Crucially, the loan does not need to be secured on the let property.

Funds can be raised by borrowing against the main residence and using the money released to fund the purchase of the buy-to-let.

By switching your mortgages around on your investment properties and main residence so more interest is paid on the rental property (which attracts tax relief), it is possible to maximise the tax relief available for borrowings. BE VERY CAREFUL BEFORE PROCEEDING.

Interest Relief

John buys four investment properties on buy-to-let mortgages, paying £100,000 each and borrowing £70,000 against each, investing £30,000 of his own money in each property.

He also has his own residential property and has a £70,000 mortgage on this.

After a few years, the investment properties are now worth £150,000 each and he remortgages these to £100,000, using the £30,000 raised on each to pay off his own mortgage and hence increase his tax relieved interest and reduce his own outgoings.

Tax relief is available for borrowings on buy to let properties up to the value of the property when first let (i.e. £100,000 per property, making it possible).

The loan does not need to be secured on the buy-to-let property, so relief would also be available if John had raised the money to buy each property by borrowing against his main residence.

Rental properties are treated as forming party of a property income business.

If you consider a balance sheet, then the total funding of the business at the start of it is assets £400,000, borrowings £280,000, capital invested by John £120,000.

In a balance sheet, this would be shown as a liability (money lent to the business by John), giving a net value at the start of the business as NIL.

This is the crucial point.

The money is 'owed' to John by the business, so when he remortgages the properties the balance sheet will not change.

The total 'liabilities' of the business will remain at £400,000, and all you have done is replace one type of borrowing (loan from John interest free) with another type of borrowing (mortgage) and released the capital which he is then free to use to repay his own mortgage (or any other purpose).

76. Interest Relief On Borrowings To Fund Businesses

With the exception of funds borrowed to fund certain Enterprise Investment Scheme shares, interest on borrowings to fund family businesses or partnerships is allowable against your income.

This point is often overlooked as funding may have been raised by way of increasing the mortgage on the family home.

It is the purpose to which the funds are put which is important here.

Interest Relief on Borrowing to Fund Business

John borrows an additional £50,000 on his main residence to provide working capital for the partnership he is involved in.

This is a qualifying loan and hence he will obtain income tax relief on the amount of interest paid on this loan.

---

77. Gilts – Tax-Free Capital Gains

Investing in index-linked Government stocks, British Government stocks or gild-edged securities (gilts) are exempt from capital gains tax. Index linked gilts can therefore be attractive, particularly to those paying capital gains at the higher rate of 28%.

Gilts – Tax-Free Capital Gains

John buys £50,000 nominal value of 3.5% Stock redeemable in 2011 at a price of £90 per £100 of nominal value.

When the Stock is repaid by the Government, he will make a profit of £5,000, which is completely tax-free.

78. Another Further Means Of Generating A Tax Free Income

Investments in zero dividend preference shares can also generate a tax free income.

This is because these are designed to increase by a set amount per annum and hence you can plan the amount of profit to be made and utilise the annual capital gains tax exemption to receive the income effectively tax free.

> **Planning to Generate a Tax Free Income**
>
> John bought a zero dividend preference share due to mature in 2012.
>
> He sells the shares and realises a profit of £8,000, which is covered by his annual exemption and as a result no tax is payable on the disposal.
>
> By buying a series of these due for repayment at different times he can plan to utilise his annual exemption and obtain a tax free 'income' over a number of years.

79. Making The Most Of A Low Income Year

You may find yourself within a tax year and know that your income is going to be substantially lower, perhaps as a deliberate move by yourself through your company or as an employee between jobs.

This can present a good opportunity to realise gains or make surrenders on single premium bonds or other investments you have.

Making the most of a Low Income Year

John is an employee and earns £150,000 per annum.

He is made redundant from his job, and is forced to take 12 months off as part of his redundancy deal. His redundancy pay is taxed in 2011/12 and provides him with sufficient income to live on for 12 months.

He will not have any income in 2012/13.

He can take this opportunity to realise capital gains.

The first £10,600 of any gains is covered by his annual exemption for the year. Gains realised in excess of the annual exemption are taxed at 18% to the extent that total income and gains does not exceed £4,370 (2012/13 figures) and at 28% thereafter.

---

80.   Distributions From Trusts

As trusts suffer from a 50% tax charge on their income, it is well worth the trustees considering making income distributions to those on the basic or 40% rates of tax. This action will generate a tax refund in the beneficiaries' hands.

The rust rate drops to 45% from 6 April 2013, so deferring income until one or after that date will reduce the tax payable by the trust.

> **Distribution from trusts**
>
> Bilal is a beneficiary of his Grandmother's Trust, and for 2012/13 has other income of £10,000.
>
> The trustees can make a distribution to him of £10,000, which is £20,000 net of 50% trust tax. He can reclaim the difference between this and the basic rate, i.e. 30%, equivalent to a tax refund of £6,000.

81. Timing Of Bonus Payments To Delay Tax

Due to the way the tax rules work, it is possible to have a deduction for a bonus declared in a set of company accounts and pay this up to nine months after the year-end.

This could be in a different tax year where other income is lower and this would result in a lower tax liability. Alternatively a deferral of the timing of the tax payment could be made.

Timing of Bonus Payments

Jane is preparing the company accounts for XYZ Ltd, her own limited company.

The company's year-end is 31 December 2011. She declares and pays a bonus for the year and receives this in August 2012.

This is when it is taxed, despite being allowed in the year ended 31 December 2011 for corporation tax purposes.

82.   Farmers Averaging

Farmers are permitted by election to average their profits over two years of assessment on a rolling basis.

This can be especially useful where one year is particularly good followed by a particularly bad one.

Farmers Averaging

John is a farmer. His profit for 2011/12 was £12,000 and his profit for 2012/13 is £50,000.

By making the election, his average profit for each of the two years becomes £31,000.

He therefore avoids the higher rate tax at 40% which would otherwise be payable on his better year.

This means that he has an overall tax saving.

---

83. Authors, Composers And Other Creative Artists

The same concept as for farmers averaging also applies for authors, composers and other creative artists to help them improve their tax position.

Authors, Composers and Other Creative Artists

Ian is an author.

The sales on his last book have slowed down and his income from sales of the book is £12,000 in 2011/12.

He launches his new book in 2012/13 to much critical acclaim, and generates a profit of £50,000 in 2012/13.

By utilising averaging, his average profit for each of the two years becomes £31,000 and he avoids the higher rate tax that would otherwise payable on his good year and saves tax overall.

---

84. Cutting Your Fuel Benefit Scale Charge

The fuel benefit charge is very expensive and in many cases you can pay more tax on the fuel than on the company car. It is therefore worthwhile to cut the fuel benefit charge.

There are two ways to do this:

Buy a new company car with a lower emissions rating or pay for your own private use petrol and reimburse the company for every drop used privately.

To make the second option work, the employee needs to be required to reimburse the full cost of all private fuel and must actually do so.

If your private mileage is low, this can be a valuable tax saving for both you and the company. Reimbursement can be made using actual costs or HMRC advisory fuel rates. This is because the current multiplier of £20,200 (2012/13 rates) used in calculating the fuel benefit means that the fuel benefit is often not worthwhile despite high pump prices.

Further, the company saves employers NIC at 13.8% on the value of the benefit and you save tax by eliminating the fuel benefit.

Cutting your Fuel Bill Charge

John runs his own company and supplies himself with a company car.

The car has CO_2 emissions of 200 g/km.

For 2012/13 the appropriate percentage is 31% and the car fuel benefit is £6,262 year (31% of £20,200).

John pays tax at the higher rate of 40%. Being supplied with fuel for his company car costs him £2,504.80 in tax for 2012/13. As a result of stricter emissions criteria and an increase in the multiplier, the cost will rise in 2013/14 and subsequent tax years. John's private mileage is low at 10,000 miles a year. He averages 40 mpg and pays about 140ppl for fuel.

This costs him around £1,589 a year for fuel.

As the actual cost of fuel for private motoring is less than the amount paid in tax (£2,504), by reimbursing the company for the cost of the private fuel, he will save £915 a year.

The company will also save Class 1A NICs of £864 (13.8% of £6,262).

85. Check Your P11D Benefits

When you receive your P11D, remember to check the benefits reported on it and query anything that does not appear right with your company straight away.

There can always be mistakes made and it always pays to check!

Also, when completing your Tax Return, ensure that you make the appropriate claim on page 2 of the Tax Return for allowable expenses to ensure you do not end up paying too much tax.

Check Your P11D benefits

John has received a P11D for a number of years and has entered the figures supplied on the form onto page 1 of his employment pages, as instructed by the P11D itself.

He now appoints an adviser, and discovers that he has overpaid several hundred pounds per year in tax as he did not complete page 2 of the employment section claiming the relevant allowable expenses.

His adviser duly helps him submit an appropriate claim and he recovers over £1,000 in overpaid tax.

86.   Claiming Relief For Expenses If You Don't Fill In A Tax Return

If you do not fill in a Tax Return you need to claim relief for expenses incurred in relation to your employment on form P87. If you do not claim the relief, you will miss out. A claim for 2012/13 must be made by 31 January 2017.

Claiming Relief for Expenses if You Don't Fill in a Tax Return

John is an employee, Each year he pays professional fees and subscriptions of £700 relevant to his job.

The subscriptions are payable to a body on HMRC's approved list. John does not receive any other benefit and does not need to submit a Tax Return.

He claims tax relief on form P87.

This is worth £140 to a basic rate taxpayer and £280 to a 40% taxpayer. Had John not claimed the relief, he would have missed out.

87. Putting Your Mobile Phone Through The Company

An employee can be provided with a mobile phone tax free. This can amount to a valuable tax-free benefit.

However, the exemption only applies if the contract for the provision of the phone is between the mobile phone provider and the company.

This is important.

If the contract is between the employee and the mobile phone provider and the employer pays the bill on the employee's behalf, the employer is regarded as settling a personal liability on the employee's behalf and this must be returned on the P11D and will be taxable as a result.

Even better, HMRC now accept that smartphones fall within the scope of the exemption.

Putting Your Mobile Phone Through The Company

John has his own company. He had a mobile phone on a £35 a month personal contract.

He cancels the contract and instead takes out a business contract in the company name, also for £35 per month.

The phone is a tax-free benefit saving John £35 per month.

The company pays £420 a year for the phone, but obtains a corporation tax deduction for this.

For a small company this is 20% (£84), reducing the net cost to the company to £336. Previously John had met the full cost of £35 per month out of his after tax income.

88. Working Abroad – Tax Free Trips For Your Family

If you are sent to work abroad for a continuous period of at least 60 days, then your employer can pay for two trips abroad per tax year for your spouse or civil partner and children without any charge to tax on the costs arising on you.

Care should be taken to space the trips out so that only two per tax year are paid for to avoid a benefit in kind charge arising.

If necessary, delay or bring forward a trip to ensure good use of this concession.

> **Tax Free Trips For Your Family**
>
> John is sent to work by his employer in Dubai for six months.
>
> His employer can pay for two trips each tax year for his wife and children.
>
> Because his work started in January 2012 he could get four trips paid for in 2012 without suffering a benefit.
>
> This is achieved by taking two trips in the 2012/12 tax year (i.e. before 6 April 2012) and two in the 2012/13 tax year (i.e. after 5 April 2012).

89. Choosing Your Accounting Date

When commencing self-employment, choosing an accounting date (the choice of year-end) can be crucial in determining whether low profits are taxed twice or high profits are taxed twice.

It will also determine the level of overlap relief carried forward and utilised on a future change of date or on cessation.

When determining and accounting date, it may be considered easiest if accounts are made up to 31 March or 5 April in the first tax year so as to eliminate any chance of an overlap profit and to maximise the period between the year-end date and the filing deadline for the Tax Return for the year.

Choosing Your Accounting Date

John starts self-employment on 1 May 2011.

He decides on a first accounting date of 30 April 2012 and annually on 30 April thereafter, as his first year is likely to create a small profit whereas he anticipates higher profits thereafter.

He will be taxed on 11 months of the first years accounting profits twice, as they form the basis of the 2011/12 tax year and also the 2012/13 tax year. If his profits are very low, then this could be of a considerable tax benefit to him.

This is because he will pay lower taxes than if he chose the 31 March year-end.

It should also be noted that his overlap relief going forward will also be correspondingly low and this could cause a problem on cessation (see tax tip Choosing A Cessation Date).

---

90. Choosing A Cessation Date

If your self-employment comes to an end, either naturally or through the decision to incorporate, then be careful as to the date you choose as this can have a major bearing on the amount of tax payable in the final year.

Choosing a Cessation Date

If John (from previous case study) chooses to cease on 31 March several years later, as his profits have grown and he is incorporating, then he will be taxed on 23 months profit in one year with very little in the way of overlap relief.

If however, he ceases on 1 May in the tax year he will be taxed on the final 12 months of profit only.

This shows that timing this decision correctly can save considerable tax.

91.   The Use Of Income Losses Generally

Whole books have been written on the use of trading losses and the why and wherefores of these.

A basic planning tip is to ensure that you are aware of the time limits for making claims and the methods of relief available.

A self-employed person making a trading loss basically has the following choices:

- this year,

- last year, (or for accounting periods ending between 24 November 2008 and 23 November 2010, the preceding three years) or

- carry forward against future profits.

The decision as to which way to go will be dependent on a number of factors including:

- future profit levels,

- other income for the year,

- the level of income for the previous year,

- the tax rates in each of those years.

The Use of Income Losses Generally

John has been in business for many years, and makes an allowable trading loss of £30,000 for the accounting period ending 30 June 2012 (which falls in the 2012/13 tax year).

His income is derived purely from his business.

The previous year's profits were £50,000, and he anticipates a profit of £20,000 the following year.

He can carry-back the loss in full to set against the profits of the previous year, recovering some tax at 40% and the balance at 20%.

92. The Loss Relief Extension to Capital Gains

Many people are unaware that if a trading loss is claimed against other income, either for the current or previous year, then by election this can be extended to capital gains, resulting in a further refund of taxes.

This can be of considerable benefit depending on the circumstances.

> **The Loss Relief Extension**
>
> John makes a loss in 2011/12 of £50,000.
>
> His income in the same year from other sources is £30,000 and he has chargeable gains (after deducting the annual exemption) of £20,000.
>
> His profit for 2012/13 is likely to be £10,000.
>
> Clearly it is advantageous in this situation to relieve the loss sideways against and extend the claim to cover the capital gains.

93. Commencement Losses

Unrepresented taxpayers frequently miss out on an additional valuable relief, which is the availability of a three year carry back for losses incurred in the opening years of a trade.

Commencement Losses

John was previously employed on a salary of £20,000 per annum, and makes a loss in his first year of trading of £20,000.

In preparation for his trade, he sold his investment property in the previous year realising a profit of £50,000.

He anticipates making a profit the following year of £10,000.

John can elect to carry this loss back three years and hence obtain tax relief on this loss at a higher rate than would otherwise be achieved.

94.   Losses And Capital Allowances

Capital allowances are treated as part of a trading loss for loss relief purposes, and so care should be taken to determine whether disclaiming these and shrinking the loss may actually leave you better off.

This is because personal allowances are ignored in loss claims, so a loss carried back could be wasted if it is set against income that is already covered by personal allowances.

Losses and Capital Allowances

John makes a loss of £30,000 including capital allowances of £5,000.

His taxable profit for the previous tax year was £30,000.

By disclaiming the capital allowances this year he will have more allowances in future years and he preserves the personal allowance in the previous year.

This means that he will save a considerable amount of tax in future years.

Similar logic can be applied in deciding whether to claim the annual investment allowance, or whether this would be wasted and it would be more beneficial to claim the writing down allowance instead.

95. Timing Your Capital Expenditure

If your cash flow allows it, consider carefully the date on which you invest in new items of plant and machinery or other items qualifying for capital allowances.

A purchase date of a few days either side of your accounting year end date can make all the difference in getting the first capital allowance in this accounting period or having to wait twelve months to get any relief for the expenditure.

Timing Your Capital Expenditures

Gordon is considering buying £10,000 worth of equipment for his business.

His year end is 31 March.

By making the purchase prior to the accounting year end date he will be able to claim allowances (either the annual investment allowance or the writing down allowance) a year earlier than if he delayed the purchase until a few days after the year end, and hence save taxes this year.

---

96.   Should I Register For VAT?

If your taxable turnover is below the VAT threshold then you may not have considered whether registering for VAT could be advantageous for you.

If you incur VAT on supplies and the majority of your customers are registered for VAT, then it may be beneficial to register for VAT on a voluntary basis.

This will allow you to recover the input tax paid on the supplies and also allow you to charge VAT on your invoices.

It will also be beneficial if many of your supplies are zero rated, such as food, as you will be able to reclaim VAT suffered and may receive a VAT repayment each quarter, which is beneficial from a cash flow perspective.

If you decide to charge VAT on your invoices then your VAT registered customers will be able to recover this amount when they next submit their VAT return.

Registering for VAT

John supplies parts to various garages, all of which are registered for VAT.

He pays input tax on all his supplies, and hence would be considerably better off by voluntarily registering for VAT and recovering this input tax.

97. The VAT Cash Accounting Scheme

If your VAT exclusive turnover is £1.35m or less, then you may account for and pay VAT on the basis of cash paid and received.

You can join this scheme at any time.

Once you are in the scheme you can continue to use it until your taxable turnover exceeds £1.6m per annum.

What this means is that you don't have to pay VAT to Customs on invoices that have not been paid yet and conversely are not allowed to claim VAT back on expenses you have incurred but not yet paid.

VAT Cash Accounting Scheme

John uses the cash accounting scheme as his turnover is below £1.35m per annum.

His major customer is having cash flow difficulties and as a result, he is not paid for his invoices totalling £100,000 until 9 months after the invoice date, at which time he accounts to Customs for the VAT due on these.

If he was not using the cash accounting scheme he would have had to account for VAT on an invoice basis and would therefore have been out of pocket to the tune of £17,500 for a period of up to nine months.

This can be enough to bring some businesses down if they do not have sufficient cash to pay this or bank facilities to fund this.

---

98. Roll-Over Relief For Business Assets

It is always worth bearing in mind that when you sell certain types of business asset, it is possible to postpone the gain by reinvesting in a qualifying asset for roll over relief purposes.

This is quite a restricted relief these days and care should be taken before relying on the availability of the relief.

The best feature about this relief is that you can claim it on more than one new purchase, and can include assets purchased one year before to three years after the date of sale of the original asset.

> **Roll-over Relief for Business assets**
>
> John sells a qualifying business asset for £100,000, making a gain of £50,000.
>
> He re-invests the entire proceeds into a new qualifying asset and the gain is entirely rolled over into the new asset.
>
> The base cost of the new asset is reduced and capital gains tax payable on the sale of the old asset is postponed.

99. Timing Your Disposals For CGT

A timing advantage of one year on the payment of tax can be achieved simply by delaying sales beyond 5 April in the tax year, so that you have use of the funds for another year and can earn interest on this money for a year longer before having to pay the tax to HMRC.

However, this needs to be balanced against a possible loss of the annual exemption if it has not been fully utilised for the earlier year.

Timing Your Disposals for CGT

John is considering selling his investment property. He has already realised gains in excess of his annual exemption.

By delaying the sale of the property until after 5 April, he will pay tax on the gain a year later and can generate some interest income on the money he has put aside for his tax liability.

100. IHT & Gifts Out Of Income

There is an exemption for inheritance tax purposes in addition to the £3,000 annual allowance for gifts, for gifts made out of income on a regular basis.

It is important to establish the regularity of the payments in order to qualify for this relief, so if gifts are made in cash then these should be regular in amount and frequency taking one year with another.

A better way of establishing regular payments may be to take out an investment policy for someone such as your (adult) child with premiums being due on a regular basis.

> **IHT Gifts out of Income**
>
> John is 50 and earns £200,000 per year.
>
> He has a son who is 25, who cannot work at present due to ill health.
>
> John, who does not need the majority of his income, wishes to gift his son £50,000 per year, but is worried about the effects this will have on his Inheritance tax bill and having to survive seven years for these monies to drop out of his estate.
>
> He establishes a quarterly standing order into his son's account, and writes a letter to his son stating that he intends to gift this amount per annum for as long as he continues to work.
>
> He continues to make the payments until his death in an accident seven years later. As he clearly established the regularity of the payments before his death, the amounts paid to his son are removed from his estate and a substantial tax saving has been achieved.

101. Make A Will

Surprisingly, many people still die intestate (i.e. without a Will).

With the ease that Wills can now be drafted and the low cost of such services, it makes good sense and can save a lot of needless heartache and stress for those left behind by making a Will, not to mention saving a lot of tax.

A simple Will gifting all your worldly goods to your spouse will avoid IHT on your entire estate, as gifts between spouses are exempt from IHT.

Making a Will

Rudolph dies intestate in 2012, leaving an estate valued at £1m. Under the Intestate rules, his wife and their children will each receive a proportion of the estate, resulting in a large IHT bill for the family.

This could easily have been avoided by making a Will and leaving property either to his spouse or to his children up to the nil rate band (£325,000).

102. BONUS TIP - Potentially Exempt Transfers

Inheritance tax is essentially a voluntary tax, in that with proper planning there is no need for your estate to pay any tax on your death.

One of the most useful tools is the potentially exempt transfer, or PET.

Under the PET rules any gift made to an individual is exempt from inheritance tax if you survive seven years from the date of the gift. If you die before seen years have elapsed, the amount charged to tax is calculated on a sliding scale, with a lower amount being taxed the longer you survive after making the gift. It is also possible to protect against the IHT liability in the interim period by taking out decreasing term assurance, which basically covers the reducing IHT liability over the seven years.

Potentially Exempt Transfers (PETs)

John makes PETs to his children Lucy and Lauren of £250,000 each in 2006.

Provided he survives until 2013, these gifts will drop out of his estate and he will have saved his estate from paying up to £200,000 on this money.

A Final Word.....

CONGRATULATIONS.....you have managed to read through all the tips.

Hopefully by reading through these practical tips you will have come across at least a few that will apply to your circumstances and save you some tax.

Or at the very least they have given you food for thought and you will take some professional advice before taking any action or refraining from any action as a result of reading these tips.

The tips are for guidance only and professional advice should always be sought before undertaking any tax planning of any sort as individual circumstances vary and other considerations may have to be taken into account before acting on these tips.

There are always more tips as tax is a very complex subject.

However I have tried to cover the more practical ideas within this book in the hope that each and every one of you acquiring this guide can take something from it.

Happy Tax Savings!

9 780956 557896